No. 82.

A CONCISE ACCOUNT OF THE RELIGIOUS SOCIETY OF FRIENDS COMMONLY CALLED QUAKERS.

PHILADELPHIA:
PUBLISHED BY THE TRACT ASSOCIATION OF FRIENDS,
No. 304 ARCH STREET.

No. 82.

A CONCISE ACCOUNT OF THE RELIGIOUS SOCIETY OF FRIENDS, COMMONLY CALLED QUAKERS.

PHILADELPHIA:
PUBLISHED BY THE TRACT ASSOCIATION OF FRIENDS,
No. 304 ARCH STREET.

A CONCISE ACCOUNT

OF THE

RELIGIOUS SOCIETY OF FRIENDS.

THE religious Society of Friends, commonly called Quakers, is a body of Christian professors, which arose in England about the middle of the seventeenth century. The civil and religious commotions which prevailed in England about this period, doubtless prepared the way for the more rapid spread of gospel truth. The fetters, in which priestcraft had long held the human mind, were beginning to be loosened; the dependence of man upon his fellow-man, in matters of religion, was shaken, and many sincere souls, panting after a nearer acquaintance with God, and a dominion over their sinful appetites and passions, which they could not obtain by the most scrupulous observance of the ceremonies of religion, were earnestly inquiring, "What must we do to be saved?" In this humble, seeking state, the Lord was graciously pleased to meet with them; sometimes without any instrumental means, at others, through the living ministry of George Fox or other anointed servants, who were prepared and sent forth to preach the gospel. The ministry of George Fox was chiefly instrumental, under the divine blessing, in convincing them of the Christian principles and testimonies which distinguish the society: and his pious labors contributed in no small degree to their establishment as an organized body, having a regular form of church government and discipline.

This devoted servant of Christ was born at Drayton, in Leicestershire, in the year 1624, and was carefully educated by his parents in the Episcopal mode of worship. He appears to have led a religious life from his childhood, and to have been deeply concerned for the salvation of his soul. Amid a high profession of religion, then generally prevalent, he observed among the people much vain and trifling conversation and conduct, as well as sordid earthly-mindedness, both which he believed to be incompatible with the Christian life. This brought great trouble upon his mind, clearly perceiving that the profession in which he had been educated did not give to its adherents that victory over sin which the gospel enjoins, and which his soul panted after. He withdrew from his former associates, and passed much of his time in retirement,— reading the Holy Scriptures, and endeavoring to wait upon the Lord for the revelation of his Spirit, to enable him rightly to understand the truths of the gospel.

In this state of reverent dependence upon the Fountain of saving knowledge, his mind was enlightened to see into the spirituality of the gospel dispensation, and to detect many errors which had crept into the professing Christian church. In the year 1647, he commenced his labors as a minister of the gospel, travelling extensively through England, generally on foot; and, from a conviction that it was contrary to Christ's positive command, he refused to receive any compensation for preaching, defraying his expenses out of his own slender means. The unction from on high, which attended his ministry, carried conviction to the hearts of many of his hearers; and his fervent disinterested labors were crowned with such success, that in a few years a large body of persons had embraced the Christian principles which he promulgated. The message of George Fox appears to have been, mainly, to direct the people to Christ Jesus, the great Shepherd and Bishop of souls, who died for them, and had sent his spirit or light into their hearts, to instruct and guide them in the things pertaining to life and salvation.

To the light of Christ Jesus, in the conscience, he and his fellow laborers in the gospel endeavored to turn the attention of all, as that by which sin was manifested and reproved, duty unfolded, and ability given to run with alacrity and joy in the way of God's commandments. The preaching of this doctrine was glad tidings of great joy to many longing souls, who eagerly embraced it, as that for which they had been seeking; and as they walked in this divine light, they experienced a growth in grace and in Christian knowledge, and gradually came to be established as pillars in the house of God.

Many of these, before they joined with George Fox, had been highly esteemed in the various religious societies of the day, for their distinguished piety and experience, being punctual in the performance of their religious duties, and regular in partaking of what are termed "the ordinances." But, notwithstanding they endeavored to be faithful to the degree of knowledge they had received, their minds were not at rest. They had not yet witnessed that redemption from sin, and that establishment in the truth, which they read of in the Bible as the privilege and duty of Christians; and hence, they were induced to believe that there was a purer and more spiritual way than they had yet found. They felt that they needed to know more of the power of Christ Jesus in their own hearts, making them new creatures, bruising Satan, and putting him under their feet, and renewing their souls up into the divine image which was lost in Adam's fall, and sanctifying them wholly, in body, soul and spirit, through the inward operations of the Holy Ghost and fire.

Great were their conflicts and earnest their prayers, that they might be brought to this blessed experience; but looking without, instead of having their attention turned within, they missed the object of their search. They frequented the preaching of the most eminent ministers; spent much time in reading the Holy Scriptures, in fasting, meditation and prayer, and increased the strictness of their lives and religious performances; but still they were not wholly freed from the dominion of sin.

Some, after wearying themselves with the multitude and severity of their duties, without finding the expected benefit from them, separated from all the forms of worship then practised, and sat down together, waiting upon the Lord, and earnestly looking and praying for the full manifestation of the kingdom and power of the Lord Jesus. Then they were brought to see that that which made them uneasy in the midst of their high profession and manifold observances, and raised fervent breathings after the God of their lives, was nothing less than the Spirit of the Lord Jesus Christ, striving with them in order to bring them out fully from under the bondage of sin, into the glorious liberty of the children of God.

They were brought to see that they had been resting too much in a mere historical belief of the blessed doctrines of the gospel, the birth, life, miracles, sufferings, death, resurrection, ascension, mediation, intercession, atonement and divinity of the Lord Jesus; but had not sufficiently looked for, and abode under, the heart-changing and sanctifying power of the Holy Spirit or Comforter; to seal those precious truths on the understanding, and give to each one a living and practical interest in them; so that they might really know Christ to be their Saviour and Redeemer, and that he had, indeed, come into their hearts and set up his righteous government there.

This was the dawning of a brighter day to their souls; and, as they attended in simple obedience to the discoveries of this divine light, they were gradually led to see further into the spirituality of the gospel dispensation. The change which it made in their views was great, and many and deep were their searchings of heart, trying "the fleece both wet and dry," ere they yielded; lest they should be mistaken and put the workings of their own imagination for the unfoldings of the Spirit of Christ; but as they patiently abode under its enlightening operations, every doubt and difficulty was removed, and they were enabled to speak, from joyful experience, of that which they had seen, and tasted, and handled of the good word of life.

The rapid spread of the doctrines preached by George Fox was surprising; and among those who embraced them were persons esteemed of the best families in the kingdom; several priests of the Episcopal denomination and ministers of other societies; besides many other learned and substantial men. There were also many in the humble walks of life, to whom excellent gifts were committed, who by faithful occupancy thereof, became eminent in turning many to righteousness. A large number of ministers, both men and women, were soon raised up in the infant society, who travelled abroad, as they believed themselves divinely called, spreading the knowledge of the truth, and strengthening and comforting the newly convinced. In a few years meetings were settled in nearly all parts of the United Kingdom; and, notwithstanding the severe persecution to which the society was subjected, by which thousands were locked up in jails and dungeons, and deprived of nearly all their property, besides being subjected to barbarous personal abuse; its members continued to increase, and manifested a zeal and devotedness which excited the admiration even of their persecutors. Their sufferings seemed only to animate them with fresh ardor, and to unite them more closely together in the bond of gospel fellowship. Instances occurred where all the parents were thrown into prison, and the children continued to hold their meetings, unawed by the threats of the officers, or the cruel whippings which some of them suffered.

As early as the year 1655, some ministers travelled on the continent of Europe, and meetings of Friends were soon after settled in Holland and other places; — some travelled into Asia, some were carried to Africa; and several were imprisoned in the Inquisitions of Rome, Malta, and in Hungary. About the same period the first Friends arrived in America, at the port of Boston, and commenced their religious labors among the people, many of whom embraced the doctrines which they heard. The spirit of persecution, from which Friends had suffered so deeply in England, made its appearance in America with increased virulence and cruelty, inflicting upon the peaceable Quakers various punishments; and finally put four of them to death by the gallows at Boston.

Notwithstanding the opposition they had to encounter, the principles of Friends continued to spread in America; many eminent ministers, actuated by the love of the gospel and a sense of religious duty, came over and travelled through the country; others removed thither and settled: — and in 1682 a large number, under the patronage of William Penn, came into the province of Pennsylvania and founded that flourishing colony. At that time meetings were settled along the Atlantic provinces, from North Carolina as far as Boston, in New England; and, at the present day, the largest body of Friends is to be found in the United States.

When we consider the great numbers who joined the society; that, without any formal admission, all those who embraced the principles of Friends and attended their meetings were considered members, as well as their children, and, of course the body in some measure implicated in the consistency of their conduct; the numerous meetings which were settled, and the wide extent of country which they embraced; it is obvious that the organization of the society would have been imperfect, without some system of church government by which the conduct of the members might be inspected and restrained.

The enlightened and comprehensive mind of George Fox was not long in perceiving the necessity for this; and he early began to make arrangements for carrying it into practice. Under the guidance of the light of Christ Jesus, which had so clearly unfolded to him the doctrines and precepts of the gospel in their true spiritual character, he commenced the arduous work of establishing meetings for discipline; and, in a few years, had the satisfaction to see his labor and concern crowned with success, both in Europe and America. Under the influence of that Christian love which warmed his heart toward the whole human family, but which more especially flowed toward the household of faith, he was very tender of the poor, and careful to see that their necessities were duly inspected and supplied. This principle has ever since characterized the society, which cheerfully supports its own poor, besides contributing its share to the public burdens. The first objects to which the attention of these meetings was directed, were the care of the poor and destitute, who had been reduced to want by persecution or other causes; the manner of accomplishing marriages; the registry of births and deaths; the education and apprenticing of children; the granting of suitable certificates of unity and approbation to ministers who travelled abroad, and the preservation of an account of the sufferings sustained by Friends in the support of their religious principles and testimonies.

It also became necessary to establish regulations for preserving the members in a line of conduct consistent with their profession. In this imperfect state of being, we are instructed from the highest authority, that offences must needs come; but it does not necessarily follow, either that the offender must be cut off from the church, or that the reproach of his misconduct should be visited upon the society to which he belongs. If, in pursuance of those Christian means laid down in the New Testament, he is brought to acknowledge and sincerely condemn his error, a brother is gained; the church is freed from reproach by his repentance and amendment of life; and thus the highest aim of all disciplinary regulations is attained. Where these effects, however, do not result from the Christian care of the church; it becomes its duty to testify against the disorderly conduct of the offender, and to declare that he has separated himself from its fellowship, and is no longer a member thereof. The views of George Fox on this subject were marked by that simplicity and scriptural soundness which distinguished his whole character.

He considered the church as a harmonious and compact body, made up of living members, having gifts differing according to the measure of grace received, yet all dependent one upon another, and each, even the weakest and lowest, having his proper place and service. As the very design of religious society is the preservation, comfort, and edification of the members, and as all have a common interest in the promotion of these great ends; he considered every faithful member religiously bound to contribute according to his capacity toward their attainment. The words of our Lord furnish a short but comprehensive description of the order instituted by Him for the government of His church: "If thy brother shall trespass against thee, go and tell his fault between thee and him alone. If he shall hear thee, thou hast gained thy brother. But if he will not hear thee, then take with thee one or two more, that in the mouth of two or three witnesses every word may be established. And if he shall neglect to hear them, tell it to the church; but if he neglect to hear the church, let him be to thee as an heathen man and a publican."

Here is no limitation of this Christian care to ministers or any other class; but any brother, who sees another offending, should, when properly qualified, admonish him in love for his good. The language of our blessed Saviour respecting the authority of his church; and his being in the midst of it in the performance of its duties, is very clear and comprehensive: "Verily I say unto you, whatsoever ye shall bind on earth, shall be bound in heaven; and whatsoever ye shall loose on earth shall be loosed in heaven. Again I say unto you, that if two of you shall agree on earth, as touching anything that they shall ask, it shall be done for them of my Father which is in heaven. For where two or three are gathered together in my name, there am I in the midst of them."

The doctrine of the immediate presence of Christ with his church, whether assembled for the purpose of divine worship, or for the transaction of its disciplinary affairs, is the foundation of all its authority.

It was on this ground that George Fox so often exhorted his fellow-believers to hold their meetings in the power of the Lord; all waiting and striving to know Christ Jesus brought into dominion in their own hearts, and his Spirit leading and guiding them in their services, that so his living presence might be felt to preside over their assemblies. In a church thus gathered, we cannot doubt, that the gracious Head condescends to be in the midst, qualifying the members to worship the Father of spirits, in spirit and in truth, or enduing them with wisdom rightly to manage the business which may engage their attention. Nor can we question that so far as they are careful to act in his wisdom and under his direction, their conclusions, being in conformity with his will, have his authority for their sanction and support.

The doctrines of the society may be briefly stated as follows. They believe in one only wise, omnipotent, and everlasting God, the creator and upholder of all things, visible and invisible; and in one Lord Jesus Christ, by whom are all things, the mediator between God and man; and in the Holy Spirit which proceedeth from the Father and the Son; one God blessed for ever. In expressing their views relative to the awful and mysterious doctrine of "the Three that bear record in heaven," they have carefully avoided the use of unscriptural terms, invented to define Him who is undefinable, and have scrupulously adhered to the safe and simple language of Holy Scripture, as contained in Matt. xxviii. 18, 19, etc.

They own and believe in Jesus Christ, the beloved and only begotten Son of God, who was conceived of the Holy Ghost, and born of the Virgin Mary. In Him we have redemption, through his blood, even the forgiveness of sins; who is the express image of the invisible God, the first-born of every creature, by whom all things were created that are in heaven or in earth, visible and invisible, whether they be thrones, dominions, principalities, or powers. They also believe that He was made a sacrifice for sin, who knew no sin, neither was guile found in his mouth; that He was crucified for mankind, in the flesh, without the gates of Jerusalem; that He was buried and rose again the third day, by the power of the Father, for our justification, and that He ascended up into heaven, and now sitteth at the right hand of God, our holy mediator, advocate, and intercessor. They believe that He alone is the redeemer and saviour of man, the captain of salvation, who saves from sin as well as from hell and the wrath to come, and destroys the works of the devil. He is the Seed of the woman that bruises the serpent's head, even Christ Jesus, the Alpha and Omega, the first and the last. He is, as the scriptures of truth say of Him, our wisdom, righteousness, justification, and redemption; neither is there salvation in any other, for there is no other name under heaven given among men whereby we may be saved.

The Society of Friends have uniformly declared their belief in the divinity and manhood of the Lord Jesus; that he was both true God and perfect man, and that his sacrifice of himself upon the cross was a propitiation and atonement for the sins of the whole world, and that the remission of sins which any partake of, is only in, and by virtue of, that most satisfactory sacrifice, and no otherwise.

Friends believe also in the Holy Spirit, or comforter, the promise of the Father, whom Christ declared He would send in his name, to lead and guide his followers into all truth; to teach them all things, and to bring all things to their remembrance. A manifestation of this Spirit they believe is given to every man to profit withal; that it convicts for sin, and, as obeyed, gives power to the soul to overcome and forsake it; it opens to the mind the mysteries of salvation, enables it savingly to understand the truths recorded in the Holy Scriptures, and gives it the living, practical, and heartfelt experience of those things which pertain to its everlasting welfare. They believe that the saving knowledge of God and Christ cannot be attained in any other way than by the revelation of this spirit;—for the apostle says, "What man knoweth the things of a man, save the spirit of man which is in him? Even so the things of God knoweth no man, but the spirit of God. Now we have received not the spirit of the world, but the spirit which is of God; that we might know the things that are freely given to us of God." If therefore the things which properly appertain to man cannot be discerned by any lower principle than the spirit of man: those things which properly relate to God and Christ, cannot be known by any power inferior to that of the Holy Spirit.

They believe that man was created in the image of God, capable of understanding the divine law, and of holding communion with his Maker. Through transgression he fell from this blessed state, and lost the heavenly image. His posterity came into the world in the image of the earthly man; and, until renewed by the quickening and regenerating power of the heavenly man, Christ Jesus, manifested in the soul, they are fallen, degenerated, and dead to the divine life in which Adam originally stood, and are subject to the power, nature, and seed of the serpent; and not only their words and deeds, but their imaginations, are evil perpetually in the sight of God. Man, therefore, in this state can know nothing aright concerning God; his thoughts and conceptions of spiritual things, until he is disjoined from this evil seed, and united to the divine light, Christ Jesus, are unprofitable to himself and to others.

But while it entertains these views of the lost and undone condition of man in the fall, the society does not believe that mankind are punishable for Adam's sin, or that we partake of his guilt, until we make it our own by transgression of the divine law.

For however early, children give evidence of the effects of the fall and of a sinful nature, they cannot be sinners from their birth, because there can be no sin where there is no transgression; and where there is not a capacity to receive a law, it cannot be transgressed. The testimony of the apostle is very positive to this point; "Where no law is there is no transgression;" "but sin is not imputed when there is no law." To account a child guilty or obnoxious to punishment, merely for an offence committed by its parents, before it could have any consciousness of being, is inconsistent both with justice and mercy; therefore no infant can be born with guilt upon its head. Those are by nature children of wrath, who walk according to the prince of the power of the air, the spirit that worketh in the hearts of the children of disobedience. Here the apostle gives their evil walking, and not anything which is not reduced to act, as a reason of their being children of wrath. Besides the natural alienation from the internal life of God, as they become capable of distinguishing the monitions of truth in their consciences, the bonds of corruption are often strengthened by habitual indulgence of the carnal propensities against the sense of duty, and thus all who have arrived at such a degree of maturity as to be convinced of right and wrong, have sinned and come short of the Glory of God.

But whatever Adam's posterity lost through him, is fully made up to them in Christ, and undoubtedly his mercy and goodness, and the extent of his propitiation, are applicable to infants, who have not personally offended, as to adults who have; and little children who are taken away before they have sinned, may with perfect confidence be resigned as entirely safe in the arms of their Saviour, who declared "of such is the kingdom of heaven."

But God, who out of his infinite love sent his Son, the Lord Jesus Christ, into the world to taste death for every man, hath granted to all men, of whatever nation or country, a day or time of visitation, during which it is possible for them to partake of the benefits of Christ's death, and be saved. For this end he hath communicated to every man a measure of the light of his own Son, a measure of grace or the Holy Spirit— by which he invites, calls, exhorts, and strives with every man, in order to save him; which light or grace, as it is received and not resisted, works the salvation of all, even of those who are ignorant of Adam's fall, and of the death and sufferings of Christ; both by bringing them to a sense of their own misery, and to be sharers in the sufferings of Christ, inwardly; and by making them partakers of his resurrection, in becoming holy, pure, and righteous, and recovered out of their sins. By which also are saved they that have the knowledge of Christ outwardly, in that it opens their understandings rightly to use and apply the things delivered in the Scriptures, and to receive the saving use of them. But this Holy Spirit, or light of Christ, may be resisted and rejected: in which then, God is said to be resisted and pressed down, and Christ to be again crucified and put to open shame; and to those who thus resist and refuse him, he becomes their condemnation.

As many as resist not the light of Christ Jesus, but receive and walk therein, it becomes in them a holy, pure, and spiritual birth, bringing forth holiness, righteousness, and purity, and all those other blessed fruits which are acceptable to God, by which holy birth, viz., Jesus Christ formed within us, and working his works in us, as we are sanctified, so we are justified in the sight of God; according to the apostle's words: "But ye are washed, but ye are sanctified, but ye are justified, in the name of the Lord Jesus, and by the Spirit of our God." Therefore, it is not by our works wrought in our will, nor yet by good works considered as of themselves, that we are justified, but *by Christ*, who is both the gift and the giver, and the cause producing the effects in us. As He hath reconciled us while we were enemies, so doth He also in his wisdom, save and justify us after this manner; as saith the same apostle elsewhere: "Not by works of righteousness which we have done, but according to his mercy He saved us, by the washing of regeneration and renewing of the Holy Ghost; which He shed on us abundantly through Jesus Christ, our Saviour, that, being justified by his grace, we should be made heirs according to the hope of eternal life." We renounce all natural power and ability in ourselves, to bring us out of our lost and fallen condition and first nature, and confess that as of ourselves we are able to do nothing that is good, so neither can we procure remission of sins or justification by any act of our own, so as to merit it, or to draw it as a debt from God due to us; but we acknowledge all to be of and from his love, which is the original and fundamental cause of our acceptance. God manifested his love toward us, in the sending of his beloved son, the Lord Jesus Christ, into the world, who gave himself an offering for us and a sacrifice to God, for a sweet-smelling savor; and having made peace through the blood of the cross, that He might reconcile us unto himself, and by the eternal Spirit, offered himself without spot unto God, He suffered for our sins, the just for the unjust, that he might bring us unto God.

In a word, if justification be considered in its full and just latitude, neither Christ's work without us, in the prepared body, nor his work within us, by his Holy Spirit, is to be excluded; for both have their place and service in our complete justification. By the propitiatory sacrifice of Christ without us, we, truly repenting and believing, are, through the mercy of God, justified from the imputation of sins and transgressions that are past, as though they had never been committed; and by the mighty work of Christ within us, the power, nature, and habits of sin are destroyed; that, as sin once reigned unto death, even so now grace reigneth, through righteousness, unto eternal life, by Jesus Christ our Lord. All this is effected, not by a bare or naked act of faith, separate from obedience, but in the obedience of faith; Christ being the author of eternal salvation to none but those that obey Him.

The Society of Friends believes that there will be a resurrection both of the righteous and the wicked; the one to eternal life and blessedness, and the other to everlasting misery and torment; agreeably to Matt. xxv. 31–46, John v. 25–29, 1 Cor. xv. 12–58. That God will judge the world by that man whom he hath ordained, even Christ Jesus the Lord, who will render unto every man according to his works; to them, who by patient continuing in well-doing during this life seek for glory and honor, immortality and eternal life; but unto the contentious and disobedient, who obey not the truth, but obey unrighteousness, indignation, and wrath, tribulation and anguish upon every soul of man that sinneth, for God is no respecter of persons.

The religious Society of Friends has always believed that the Holy Scriptures were written by divine inspiration, and contain a declaration of all the fundamental doctrines and principles relating to eternal life and salvation; and that whatsoever doctrine or practice is contrary to them, is to be rejected as false and erroneous; that they are a declaration of the mind and will of God, in and to the several ages in which they were written, and are obligatory on us, and are to be read, believed, and fulfilled by the assistance of divine grace. Though it does not call them "the Word of God," believing that epithet peculiarly applicable to the Lord Jesus; yet it believes them to be the words of God, written by holy men as they were moved by the Holy Ghost; that they were written for our learning, that we, through patience and comfort of the Scriptures, might have hope; and that they are able to make wise unto salvation, through faith which is in Christ Jesus. It looks upon them as the only fit outward judge and test of controversies among Christians, and is very willing that all its doctrines and practices should be tried by them, freely admitting that whatsoever any do, pretending to the spirit, which is contrary to the Scriptures, be condemned as a delusion of the devil.

As there is one Lord and one faith, so there is but one baptism, of which the water baptism of John was a figure. The baptism which belongs to the gospel, the Society of Friends believes, is "not the putting away the filth of the flesh, but the answer of a good conscience toward God, by the resurrection of Jesus Christ." This answer of a good conscience can only be produced by the purifying operation of the Holy Spirit, transforming and renewing the heart, and bringing the will into conformity to the divine will. The distinction between Christ's baptism and that of water is clearly pointed out by John: "I indeed baptize you with water unto repentance, but he that cometh after me is mightier than I, whose shoes I am not worthy to bear, he shall baptize you with the Holy Ghost and fire, whose fan is in his hand, and he will thoroughly purge his floor and gather his wheat into the garner, but he will burn up the chaff with unquenchable fire."

In conformity with this declaration, the society holds that the baptism which now saves is inward and spiritual; that true Christians are "baptized by one Spirit into one body;" that "as many as are baptized into Christ have put on Christ;" and that "if any man be in Christ, he is a new creature: old things are passed away, behold all things are become new, and all things of God."

Respecting the communion of the body and blood of our Lord Jesus Christ, the Society of Friends believes, that it is inward and spiritual — a real participation of his divine nature through faith in him, and obedience to the power of the Holy Ghost, by which the soul is enabled daily to feed upon the flesh and blood of our crucified and risen Lord, and is thus nourished and strengthened. Of this spiritual communion, the breaking of bread and drinking of wine by our Saviour with his disciples was figurative; the true Christian supper being that set forth in the Revelations: "Behold, I stand at the door and knock; if any man hear my voice and open the door, I will come in to him and will sup with him, and he with me."

As the Lord Jesus declared, "Without me ye can do nothing," the Society of Friends holds the doctrine that man can do nothing that tends to the glory of God and his own salvation without the immediate assistance of the Spirit of Christ; and that this aid is especially necessary in the performance of the highest act of which he is capable, even the worship of the Almighty. This worship must be in spirit and in truth; an intercourse between the soul and its great Creator, which is not dependent upon, or necessarily connected with, anything which one man can do for another. It is the practice therefore of the society to sit down in solemn silence to worship God; that each one may be engaged to gather inward to the gift of divine grace, in order to experience ability reverently to wait upon the Father of spirits, and to offer unto Him through Christ Jesus our holy Mediator, a sacrifice well pleasing in his sight, whether it be, in silent mental adoration, the secret breathing of the soul unto Him, the public ministry of the gospel, or vocal prayer or thanksgiving. Those, who are thus gathered, are the true worshippers, "who worship God in the spirit, rejoice in Christ Jesus, and have no confidence in the flesh."

In relation to the ministry of the gospel, the society holds that the authority and qualification for this important work are the special gift of Christ Jesus, the great Head of the church, bestowed both upon men and women, without distinction of rank, talent, or learning; and must be received immediately from Him, through the revelation of his spirit in the heart; agreeably to the declarations of the apostle: "He gave some apostles, and some prophets, and some evangelists, and some pastors and teachers, for the perfecting of the saints, for the work of the ministry, for the edifying of the body of Christ"— "to one is given by the Spirit, the word of wisdom, to another the word of knowledge, by the same Spirit; to another faith; to another the gifts of healing — to another the working of miracles — to another prophecy — to another discerning of spirits; to another divers kinds of tongues; to another the interpretation of tongues; —

but all these worketh that one and the self-same Spirit, dividing to every man severally as he will." "If any man speak, let him speak as the oracles of God; if any man minister, let him do it as of the ability which God giveth; that God in all things may be glorified through Jesus Christ."

Viewing the command of our Saviour, "Freely ye have received, freely give," as of lasting obligation upon all his ministers, the society has, from the first, steadfastly maintained the doctrine that the gospel is to be preached without money and without price, and has borne a constant and faithful testimony, through much suffering, against a man-made hireling ministry, which derives its qualification and authority from human learning and ordination; which does not recognize a direct divine call to this solemn work, or acknowledge its dependence, for the performance of it, upon the renewed motions and assistance of the Holy Spirit. Where a minister believes himself called to religious service abroad, the expense of accomplishing which is beyond his means, if his brethren unite with his engaging in it and set him at liberty therefor, the meeting he belongs to is required to see that the service be not hindered for want of pecuniary means.

The Society of Friends believes that war is wholly at variance with the spirit of the gospel, which continually breathes peace on earth and good-will to men. That, as the reign of the Prince of peace comes to be set up in the hearts of men, nation shall not lift up sword against nation, neither shall they learn war any more. They receive, in their full signification, the plain and positive command of Christ: "I say unto you that ye resist not evil,"—"love your enemies; bless them that curse you, do good to them that hate you, and pray for them that despitefully use you and persecute you, that ye may be the children of your

Father which is in heaven." They consider these to be binding on every Christian, and that the observance of them would eradicate from the human heart those malevolent passions in which strife and warfare originate.

In the same manner the society believes itself bound by the express command of our Lord: "Swear not at all," and that of the apostle James: "But above all things, my brethren, swear not; neither by heaven, neither by earth, neither by any other oath; but let your yea be yea, and your nay nay, lest ye fall into condemnation;" and therefore its members refuse, for conscience sake, either to administer or to take an oath.

Consistently with its belief in the purity and spirituality of the gospel, the society cannot conscientiously unite in the observance of public fasts, and feasts, and holy days, set up in the will of man. It believes that the fast we are called to, is not bowing the head as a bulrush for a day, and abstaining from meats or drinks; but a continued fasting from every thing of a sinful nature, which would unfit the soul for being the temple of the Holy Ghost. It holds that under the gospel dispensation there is no inherent holiness in any one day above another, but that every day is to be kept alike holy; by denying ourselves, taking up our cross daily and following Christ. Hence it cannot pay a superstitious reverence to the first day of the week; but inasmuch as it is necessary that some time should be set apart to meet together to wait upon God, and as it is fit that at some times we should be freed from other outward affairs, and as it is reasonable and just that servants and beasts should have some time allowed them for rest from their labor; and as it appears that the apostles and primitive Christians used the first day of the week for these purposes: the society, therefore, observes this day as a season of cessation from all unnecessary labor, and for religious retirement and waiting upon God; yet not so as to prevent them from meeting on other days of the week for divine worship.

The society has long borne a testimony against the crying sin of enslaving the human species, as entirely at variance with the commands of our Saviour, and the spirit of the Christian religion; and likewise against the unnecessary use of intoxicating liquors.

Friends believe magistracy or civil government to be God's ordinance, the good ends thereof being for the punishment of evil-doers, and the praise of them that do well. While they feel themselves restrained by the pacific principles of the gospel from joining in any warlike measures to pull down, set up, or defend any particular government: they consider it a duty to live peaceably under whatever form of government it shall please Divine Providence to permit to be set up over them; to obey the laws so far as they do not violate their consciences; and, where an active compliance would infringe on their religious principles, to endure patiently the penalties imposed upon them. The society discourages its members from accepting posts or offices in civil government which expose them to the danger of violating our Christian testimonies against war, oaths, etc., and also from engaging in political strife and party heats and disputes, believing that the work to which we are particularly called, is to labor for the spread of the peaceful reign of the Messiah.

It also forbids its members to go to law with each other; enjoining them to settle their disputes, if any arise, through the arbitration of their brethren; and if peculiar circumstances, such as the cases of executors, trustees, etc., render this course impracticable or unsafe, and liberty is obtained to bring the matter into court, that they should on such occasions, as well as in suits with other persons, conduct themselves with moderation and forbearance, without anger or animosity; and in their whole demeanor evince that they are under the government of a divine principle, and that nothing but the necessity of the case brings them there.

In conformity with the precepts and examples of the apostles and primitive believers, the society enjoins upon its members a simple and unostentatious mode of living, free from needless care and expense; moderation in the pursuit of business; and that they discountenance lotteries of every kind, music, dancing, stage-plays, horse-races, and all other vain and unprofitable amusements; as well as the changeable fashions and manners of the world, in dress, language, or the furniture of their houses; that, daily living in the fear of God and under the power of the cross of Christ, which crucifies to the world and all its lusts, they may show forth a conduct and conversation becoming their Christian profession, and adorn the doctrine of God our Saviour in all things.

NOTE.—Those who desire further knowledge of the principles and practices of the religious Society of Friends, are referred to *George Fox's Journal, Barclay's Apology, Phipps on the Original and Present State of Man, Penn's Rise and Progress of the People called Quakers, Dymond on War, Penn's No Cross No Crown,* and numerous other standard works which may be had at Friends' Bookstore, No. 304 Arch Street, Phila.

www.ingramcontent.com/pod-product-compliance
Lightning Source LLC
LaVergne TN
LVHW011140110826
845150LV00008B/2424
* 9 7 8 1 4 1 8 1 9 2 7 9 2 *